Starting wi̇ Choice

Inclusive strategies for consulting young children

Mary Dickins, Sue Emerson and Pat Gordon-Smith

 Save the Children

Save the Children fights for children in the UK and around the world who suffer from poverty, disease, injustice and violence. We work with them to find lifelong answers to the problems they face.

Save the Children UK is a member of the International Save the Children Alliance, the world's leading independent children's rights organisation, with members in 27 countries and operational programmes in more than 100.

Published by
Save the Children
1 St John's Lane
London EC1M 4AR
UK

First published 2004, reprinted 2005, 2006

© The Save the Children Fund 2004

Registered Charity No. 213890

ISBN 1 84187 085 4

Edited by Pat Gordon-Smith
Design: Neil Adams
Illustrations: Bethan Matthews
Cover design: Joely Merrington
Printed by Biddles, King's Lynn, Norfolk

Contents

Acknowledgements   v

Introduction   1
Settings involved in the CHOOSE project   2
    Anansi Nursery, Harlesden   2
    John Smith Centre, Tower Hamlets   2

1 The right to be consulted   4
Young disabled children   6
Inclusion   8

2 Guidance for consulting young children   11
Listening to children   13
    Consultation techniques   17
    Interviews   17
    Projective techniques   18
    Drawing what you want to say   21
    Giving an opinion   22
    Ranking preferences   24
    Mapping   25
Ideas for giving children choice   27
    Buying toys and equipment   27
    Going on an outing   29
    Employing several techniques in one consultation   30
The Foundation Stage – implications for choice   32

3 Involving parents   35

4 Staff training and support   39

Outline content for staff training   40
   Principles   40
   Policy and practice   41
Consulting staff   42
   Principles for effective consultation with staff   42

References   45

Acknowledgements

The authors dedicate this publication to *all* early years workers and managers who are striving to make inclusion a reality.

We would like to thank the managers, staff, children and parents from the Anansi Children's Centre (Harlesden), John Smith Family Centre (Tower Hamlets) and Copenhagen Area Sure Start (Islington) for working with us, sharing their practice and showing the value of including young children in planning and decision-making.

Introduction

This guide is published at a time when the inclusion of disabled children in mainstream education is at last being recognised in government policy. This is greatly to be welcomed, but it is vital that we get inclusion right if it is to be of real benefit to all children.

A very clear obstacle in the way of full inclusion is that, as a society and as early years practitioners, we still have a tendency to do things *for* young disabled children rather than helping them develop the skills they need to achieve more independence.

Starting with Choice is the culmination of the Save the Children CHOOSE project, which sought to challenge the assumption that young disabled children lack the ability to make effective choices about their needs. Staff from Save the Children had previously been involved in projects with early years settings to promote young children's participation, and these had highlighted some concerns about ensuring that practice was genuinely inclusive (Fajerman, Jarrett & Sutton, 2000).

In the course of the CHOOSE project, we worked with two early years settings in London to find ways of helping young disabled children to develop decision-making skills. We were keen to find workable solutions for all the children and staff at these settings, but were careful to address the particular needs of children with physical and learning difficulties in making personal choices about their care and education. To achieve this, we looked for activities that would stretch individual experience, and strategies for ensuring that *everyone* could participate in decisions for the whole group.

This book draws on these experiences, presenting examples and guidelines for other early years practitioners who want to make inclusion part of their work with children.

Settings involved in the CHOOSE project

Anansi Nursery, Harlesden

This local authority setting opened about 30 years ago in a residential area of Brent in north-west London. The nursery occupies purpose-built accommodation with adjacent gardens. The setting provides an integrated service for children of all abilities and is registered for 40 two-to-five-year-olds. At the time of our visit, 25 children attended the setting and 75 per cent of them had special educational needs. Eleven staff worked with three groups of children who attended between six and ten sessions weekly.

John Smith Centre, Tower Hamlets

In 2000, Ofsted reported: "John Smith Children's Resource Centre is a local authority children's centre registered with the London Borough of Tower Hamlets. Established in 1994, the centre is housed in purpose-built accommodation and in 1996 became an integrated service for children with severe learning difficulties and special educational needs. The centre caters for a culturally and linguistically diverse local community, predominantly Bangladeshi but including those from African-Caribbean, Pakistani, Moroccan, mixed race and white British parentage. The staff team reflects the local community and in total speaks eight different languages." (Ofsted, 2000)

When we visited, there were ten members of staff working in the early years section, where there were ten children with either severe learning difficulties or physical disabilities. The centre's community provision offered a weekly drop-in and a parent/carers' toddler group which had 1,250–1,500 users each month. The community group also hosted a Bangladeshi mothers' support group and a childminders' drop-in.

1 The right to be consulted

Everyone should have the right to give their opinion on matters which affect them, and young children are no exception. While they may not use lengthy, reasoned argument, all young children can express very clear preferences as long as they are asked to do so in ways that they understand, and can respond using methods which are appropriate for their age and skills.

The right of young children to be consulted where decisions affect them is enshrined in the United Nations Convention on the Rights of the Child (CRC), which was ratified by the UK government in 1991.

Article 12 of the CRC says that all children who are capable of forming their own views have the right to express them freely in all matters affecting them, and that their opinions should be given due weight in accordance with their age or maturity. The last phrase puts a duty on adults to use their judgement in consulting children of different ages and converting their views to actions. It does not question the right of young children to be heard.

Underpinning a children's rights approach is the idea that all children have the right to feel good about themselves. Positive self-esteem has been shown by countless researchers to be a crucial factor in successful learning, and knowing that your views are both listened to and acted upon is fundamental to developing a strong sense of self-worth.

Experience shows that young children can express preferences and that they benefit from doing so (see box, 'Outdoor choice at Anansi'). Given that, the only right and sensible thing to do is to help them learn how to voice their opinions effectively.

Outdoor choice at Anansi

Staff at Anansi Nursery decided to consult the children to identify their preferred outdoor play activities, plan the physical layout of the outdoor provision and provide the very best outdoor environment for all the children.

The consultation involved several techniques, such as offering different practical and natural resources (bamboo, gravel, long grass, a mini-beast area) to find out which the children enjoyed most, and asking them to point to areas on a map of the garden to see which they liked best (see pages 30–32 for more details).

Anansi has two gardens; one in front and one at the back. The children were invited to say which garden they preferred and offered very clear views, both positive and negative. One child said: "I like the pre-school garden better because there are no boys." Another said: "We must not shout because it hurts the old people's ears [in a building next door]." One child repeatedly signed 'tree' in Makaton and located the flash card with a picture of the tree, indicating her desire to be taken to the back garden. Staff helped her to climb the tree, where she stayed for half an hour.

Young disabled children

The right of young disabled children to be consulted over decisions affecting them is included in the right of *all* children to be consulted. This is stated quite clearly under Article 2 of the CRC, which says that the rights given in the Convention apply to all children equally, irrespective of their race, sex, religion, disability, opinion or family background. Article 23 further protects the rights of disabled children, stating that they should enjoy conditions which promote independence and enable them to participate actively in the community.

While the CRC has been recognised by the UK Government, it is not law. There are no enforceable laws in the UK stating that disabled children should be consulted. However, the 2001 revision of the Special Educational Needs Code of Practice *does* state that the views of children with special educational needs should be sought and taken into account, while the 1996 Education Act and Nursery and Grant-Maintained Schools Act place a duty on all schools and other providers receiving the nursery education grant to 'have regard to' the Code.

In order to express their views, all young children need to acquire important decision-making skills, and there are reasons to be particularly concerned that young disabled children should be given the opportunities to do this.

Disabled children are subject to a higher degree of adult intervention than other children, so their scope for making day-to-day choices is often severely limited. Furthermore, they frequently encounter distressing situations where any individual would wish their voice to be heard: they are statistically more vulnerable to abuse than non-disabled children, are more likely to receive medical interventions and treatments, and to be subject to various kinds of assessment procedures. Parents and practitioners are more likely to regard themselves as advocates for disabled children, and where children have specific communication difficulties they are less likely to be consulted.

With so many obstacles in their way, it is vital that young disabled children are given an equal chance to gain the skills for effective participation at the earliest opportunity. Changes made at the John Smith Centre illustrate what can be done and the speed at which young children – even those with severe disabilities – can benefit (see box, 'Making things accessible').

Making things accessible

Staff at the John Smith Centre wanted to tackle some of the design problems in their building which prevented free access to play equipment.

All the creative equipment was put in one room so that most materials were on low shelves and completely accessible to all the children. The children were then given free choice of play activity using whichever materials they wished. This is consultation in its simplest form.

Once they were used to the new layout Tabitha and William soon began to put out items from the shelves and to ask for other things they knew to be in cupboards. Their choices of activities were completely different from the ones which had been planned for them.

Azizur, who has global delays, did not initially react to the new accessible layout and would only use materials put out on the tables by staff. He was unsure how to react even when encouraged to take the materials that he wanted. But just one week after the changes were made, Azizur broke off from drawing with pencils that had been set up by staff, put them down and went to a shelf. He selected a crayon and a different colour paper, then used the crayon for a while before returning to the shelf and choosing several more.

The effect of having been given free choice became very clear when the staff at John Smith decided to change the seating arrangements for lunch but didn't mention it to the children in advance. This new layout was met with disapproval and some refusal to sit down. There were very sullen faces. Staff were left in no doubt that the children had become used to being asked for their preferences, and felt positive about it. They were now unhappy at having something imposed on them.

Inclusion

"Inclusive education enables all students to fully participate in any mainstream early years provision, school, college or university. Inclusive education provision has training and resources aimed at fostering every student's equality and participation in all aspects of the life of the learning community."

(Reiser, Chapman & Skitteral, 2002)

When talking about involving young children in making decisions, it is important to look at the kind of environment in which *all* children can be consulted effectively. Early years settings which operate inclusive policies certainly work best for disabled children, but they are also effective in consulting non-disabled children. This is because inclusion is not just about educating disabled children, it is concerned with quality provision for everyone. The nine guiding principles of inclusive education, adopted by the Alliance for Inclusive Education in March 2002, are founded in fundamental respect for all individuals:

1. A person's worth is independent of their abilities or their achievements.

2. Every human being is able to feel and think.

3. Every human being has a right to communicate and be heard.

4. All human beings need each other.

5. Real education can only happen in the context of real relationships.

6. All people need support and friendship from people their own age.

7. Progress for all learners is achieved by building on things people can do rather than on what they can't.

8. Diversity brings strength to all living systems.

9. Collaboration is preferable to competition.

Critics of inclusion fear that including disabled children will somehow 'dilute' the educational achievements of schools. But there is increasing evidence to suggest that inclusion improves the achievement of all children, whether or not they are disabled. Schools developing inclusive education are concerned to maintain or improve the academic performance of their pupils while simultaneously meeting greater diversity. The general lack of information about the performance of children with special educational needs (SEN) is flagged up by the Audit Commission (2002): "Schools have difficulty setting reasonable targets and knowing what constitutes reasonable progress. Most local education authorities are not monitoring outcomes for pupils with SEN or analysing their performance separately."

However, evidence is emerging, particularly from the London Borough of Newham, which suggests that an inclusive approach to education can raise standards overall. "Pupils with identified difficulties or disabilities appear to benefit educationally from schools developing inclusive education… Pupils who do not have identified difficulties appear to attain as well or better and make the same or more progress in classes developing inclusive education as they do in traditional mainstream classes." (Sebba with Sachdev, 1998)

In the early years sector it has been widely accepted as good practice for pre-school children to attend mainstream provision wherever possible. The SEN Code of Practice 2001 confirms this consensus in its guidance that the requirements of children with special educational needs should be met in mainstream settings.

Because nurseries and playgroups are generally smaller, more manageable institutions, it is often easier for them to achieve the basic conditions for successful inclusion. Effective inclusion in the early years offers potential benefits for everyone:

- Disabled children benefit from contact with their non-disabled peers in terms of communication skills and social and emotional development.

- Parents can become fuller members of their local communities and suffer less from the isolation that segregated services can bring.

- Families who have had a positive pre-school experience are more likely to opt for mainstream provision at the primary school stage.

- Staff and non-disabled children benefit from the change in attitude that familiarity and acceptance can bring: they learn to look beyond the disability to each unique and valuable person. (Dickins with Denziloe, 2003)

2 Guidance for consulting young children

The good news for children, practitioners and managers is that strategies, methods and approaches aimed at consulting and supporting disabled children in early years settings are good for *all* children. Measures which increase accessibility to any kind of learning usually enrich the curriculum and the depth of experiences for all children. For example, activities which appeal to all five senses – and which are therefore more accessible to children who experience difficulties with one or more of their senses – automatically offer a richer and more enjoyable experience for any child.

The following guidelines for effective consultation apply when working with any young child. Where points refer directly to disabled children, they are usually an extension of a more general principle.

- Very young children can be consulted, so long as the consultation is carefully planned and supported.

- Children with complex and multiple disabilities can participate effectively and have a right to do so. It is up to practitioners to find the right way of listening, as there are few children who cannot say 'yes' or 'no' in some way with regard to some issue, item or approach which affects them and has an impact on their life.

- No child should be forced to take part in a consultation if they really do not wish to do so.

- All young children need adult guidance to enable them to express their views. Find out what the children need to know in order to make an informed decision, and fill in any gaps before beginning a consultation.

- Consultation methods must be participatory, enjoyable, negotiable and responsive to children's ideas. Where possible, involve children in planning the consultation as they will provide valuable insights, helping you to ask the right questions.

- Be clear about why you are consulting children and what you are consulting them about.

- Listen carefully to the children's views and concerns, and take them into account (see below). Plan in advance how to process and use the information you get from the children.

- Try wherever possible to use children's own words, and avoid adult interpretation.

- This kind of work should not be undertaken unless the adults involved are aspirational, prepared to share power and wish to promote positive change. If consultation of young disabled children is to be successful, it is crucial that settings already recognise the importance of anti-discriminatory practice, provide access to a full curriculum and work in partnership with children, parents and each other towards inclusive goals.

- Give feedback to children on how their views have influenced decisions or been used.

Listening to children

A good consultation requires adults who listen to young children, who take the time to understand what they mean and are willing to act on their views. Research shows that, regardless of culture or language spoken, ability or disability, 55 per cent of communication is non-verbal; only 7 per cent is verbal (words only) and 38 per cent is vocal (including tone of voice, inflection and other sounds). (Mehrabian, 1971)

This means that 'listening' must be defined in the widest way possible as being tuned into all the messages children are giving out. Here are some fairly simple techniques that will help you to be an effective listener.

- Always make eye contact and get down to the child's level.

- Show interest in everything the child has to say, using your judgement later on to draw out the information you actually need for future planning.

- Give children time and try not to interrupt or finish sentences.

- Don't attempt to fill every silence.

- When the child has finished talking, sum up what he/she has said and reflect it back to him/her, for example: "It sounds like you felt very angry when Tommy took your ball away."

- Don't feel that you have to have an answer or a solution for everything.

- Acknowledge the feelings that are being expressed and give them validity.

- Avoid closed questions that leave you open to a yes/no answer. (For example: "Are there things you like at nursery?") Use open-ended questions instead. (For example: "Tell me some of the things you like about nursery.")

- Remember that 'why?' questions can sound like an accusation.

- Talk respectfully to children; they know when they are being patronised.

- Be honest if you don't know something.

- If you make a mistake, apologise.

In addition, when listening to disabled children, it is important to understand their preferred method of communication and, if necessary, to work with an interpreter or someone who knows them well. For more information about possible methods of communication, see the box 'Communication techniques for disabled children'.

Communication techniques for disabled children

Adapted from *Side by Side: Guidelines for inclusive play* (Kidsactive, 2000).

Establish the basic principles:

- Get as much information as you can from parents, professionals and other carers about how the child communicates, and the equipment needed.
- Establish the child's means of communicating 'yes' and 'no'.
- Incorporate a range of *familiar* objects to help the child (toys, photographs etc).

Blissymbols were developed as an alternative means of communication for children with cerebral palsy. A child using Bliss will have their own board or chart with a range of symbols appropriate to their needs. They may indicate the symbols they wish to use in a variety of ways, such as pointing or eye movements.

Braille is a method of reading by touch used by people with visual impairments, usually written on a machine called a Brailler which is like a typewriter but only has six keys. The Royal National Institute for the Blind run a translation service.

British Sign Language (BSL) is the sign language used by the deaf community in Britain. It has a structure and grammar that is different to English and cannot be used at the same time as spoken English.

Cued speech is used alongside lip reading, to help children understand what they are seeing on the lips. The system has a series of hand shapes to represent consonants and positions around or near the mouth that can be touched to represent vowels. The system is particularly useful in helping children distinguish words that look very similar when they are lip reading.

Deafblind manual alphabet is designed for people who are deaf and blind, and whose understanding can only be reached through the sense of touch. The speaker presses the various signs of this alphabet onto the deaf-blind person's hand.

continued overleaf

continued from previous page

Electronic communication uses speech synthesisers and digitised speech machines linked to computers to aid communication. While there is no automatic entitlement to these devices on the NHS, there is a national network of communication aids centres, usually attached to hospitals, which will make free assessments.

Lip reading is the ability to read the patterns that people make with their lips when they speak.

Makaton uses signs (gestures) and symbols (pictures) depicting selected concepts to help hearing people who have learning and communication difficulties. There is a core vocabulary of 450 signs and symbols, each representing a basic concept, which can be further supported by signs and symbols representing up to 7,000 other concepts. Makaton is an aid to communication, not a language in itself. Signs and symbols are used in the order they would be spoken in English, and are accompanied by spoken English.

Paget Gorman signed speech is a sign system used at the same time as spoken language to make clear the structure of the English language. Its primary function is educational: to develop an understanding of the use of language and to give access to written and spoken English. It is used mainly with children who have specific speech and language disorders.

Signed English consists of signs taken from BSL, together with specially developed signs which are only used in signed English. It is designed to be used at the same time as spoken English rather than separately from it.

Total communication stresses the importance of using all possible communication methods equally if a child with hearing loss is to gain an understanding of language – so, for instance, sign language would be combined with lip reading.

Consultation techniques

Consultation with young children should not be a one-off thing, and it needn't be something you do only rarely: after all, consultation extends to the simple practice of offering children a free choice between listening to one story or another in the book corner.

There are lots of different ways to consult young children more formally. You can use a combination of them in the course of one consultation, or use different methods when you wish to find out different things. Here are some ideas.

Interviews

Use interviews when you want to find out simple details, perhaps at the beginning of a longer consultation. Interviews can be videoed or tape-recorded, or carried out using written questionnaires, in which case the practitioner involved will write down the children's answers. In some cases, the children may wish to interview each other. Interviews can be carried out with individuals, pairs or groups, and can be repeated after an agreed period of time to see if the children's opinions have changed.

Issues to bear in mind when using this technique:

- Do not go straight into an interview. Take some time to explain its purpose, building up trust in the process.

- Design the questions carefully so that the children understand them fully. It is a good idea to pilot them with one or two children first to see if the level of difficulty is right.

- Know how the children prefer to communicate and make sure you have the necessary skills, or work through a signer or interpreter.

- Devise a way for the children to end the interview if they wish, and ensure they understand it.

The strength of this technique is that the children can tell you what they think is important, and this immediately shows them that their views are valued. It is particularly useful for children who do not feel comfortable taking part in large discussions or circle times.

Its weakness is that it can take a lot of time, as interviews tend to work best when carried out with pairs of children or small groups. It can also yield a huge amount of information that is difficult to process.

The technique can be adapted for children with language or motor impairment by providing picture cards to represent the options available.

A nursery in Islington interviewed children about their food preferences at snack and tea times. Pictures represented the choices available and they were displayed by food group (carbohydrates, fruit and vegetables, and so on). The children chose something from each food group to ensure a balance to their meals. The older children recorded the preferences of the younger children, and even very young children and those with language impairments were able to take part. Less popular combinations were occasionally offered, but with alternatives. The nursery reported more interest from the children and less waste. (Fajerman, Jarrett & Sutton, 2000)

Projective techniques

These techniques make use of persona dolls, and are particularly effective with younger children. A persona doll has its own name and personal history, which stay the same with each child and across different play sessions. Persona dolls allow you to introduce somebody new into the setting, someone who can help the children to see things from different points of view or who can listen to them in different ways. They need not be specially made, and might be a puppet, a storyboard character or a teddy bear.

In the projective technique, a persona doll is introduced to a group of children and its character is established during a short 'conversation'. The children can find out more about the doll by asking it questions, and the doll asks the children questions to find out more about them. This is particularly useful if you suspect that children may not be comfortable with responding to direct questions about their views. For instance, children may be happy to tell you what they like about their setting, but may not be so forthcoming about their dislikes. A persona doll can be a naïve character who needs to find out about the whole world, and so might ask a question like: "What do children dislike about this room?" Children feel more comfortable responding to this sort of question because they are answering in a general way. However, their individual views can appear very clearly in this way. This technique has been used successfully to discuss very difficult topics, such as

In 1998, the Daycare Trust used teddy bears in conversations with 45 children in three nurseries, to find out what they liked and disliked about their setting. The teddy bears wanted to know what the children thought about friends, what food was good, how you had fun outside and what was the best thing to play with. And the children responded with lots of detail. For example, when talking about having lunch at nursery, Samuel told the teddy bear: "It is fun, my friends always sit next to me."

Samuel's comment, and many others like them, helped the Daycare Trust draw conclusions about what children liked most about their daycare. Once all the children's responses had been gathered together, the information was published in a guide for parents called Listening to Children, which is aimed at helping parents find out if a daycare setting will suit their child. (Daycare Trust, 1998)

Parents are directed towards useful questions they can ask daycare providers, so Samuel's ideas about food are echoed in the suggested questions: "Are mealtimes fun for children?" and, "Can children choose who they sit with at mealtimes?"

smacking, child abuse and racism. The technique works best with small groups, and can be run by an adult or an older child.

Issues to bear in mind when using the projective technique:

- You need to have worked out the doll's personality and background details before introducing it to the children.

- Some children react best to dolls that are more lifelike and others prefer fantasy characters; there is no rule as to what will work best.

- Plan how to record the responses, summarise and present the results. To be sure that quotes are accurate and that you capture the children's input, it may be necessary to have another adult present whose role is only to record what is said, or to use a tape recorder (although some children can be distracted by this). Make summaries at regular intervals and check them with the children and adults who were present, to be sure they reflect the discussion. Wherever possible, written summaries should use the children's own words and phrasing.

The strength of the projective technique is that it can allow children to put some emotional distance between themselves and what is being said: they can talk about how they think the character would feel and not about their own feelings. Alternatively, they can talk to the character 'child to child', which is sometimes less scary than talking to an adult.

The weakness of this technique is that the introduction of the character can be distracting. For best results, a character should be introduced over a period of time, so the children can get used to it. Use this time to talk with the children about everyday things and move on to more demanding issues later.

As all persona dolls have their own character, it is very simple to introduce dolls with a range of disabilities, to ensure that all children have someone they can identify with or can find out more about. An inclusive setting would have such dolls even where there are no disabled children in attendance. Children who sign or use other communication aids can also join in developing the stories.

Drawing what you want to say

In this form of consultation, the children draw a picture or build a model describing what they think. As previously, adults can capture any words the children want to say about their work on labels to go on the piece of art. This can be particularly useful if you want children's opinions on the layout of a room or outdoor space. It is lots of fun for very young children and is also very good for children who don't, or can't, use words.

This technique requires that everyone, including the children, should be clear about the distinction between drawings made as part of a consultation and those used for therapeutic art.

The strength of this technique is that it is usually easy to introduce, as the children are already used to drawing and modelling.

A weakness is that it can be difficult to interpret what the children have drawn or made. Sometimes this can be dealt with by talking to the children about what they have made, and why, but getting a clear interpretation can be difficult when working with some disabled children, and the technique may not always be suitable.

> In a consultation about children's view of health and health services, conducted by Save the Children for the NHS Executive (London), some children chose to draw their responses. This highlighted quite complex relationships with doctors and dentists that could then be explored further in discussion groups. For example, most children seemed to have a relatively positive relationship with their dentist. In fact, one child drew herself skipping into the dental surgery, shouting 'Yippee'. Others talked about collecting stickers and colouring sheets to take home. However, one child drew the cabinet and drawer where the dentists kept their tools and the caption wished that it would be kept shut when he went into the surgery so that he could not see them. The drawings freed up other children to share their views, good and bad.

Giving an opinion

The first few times you get opinions from children it is best to offer them a choice between just two possible answers. For example, the question: "Did you like having the water tray outside yesterday?" will lead the children to respond either 'yes' or 'no'. This is easier for children who are not used to being asked for their opinion. The technique can be adapted in all sorts of ways that the children will enjoy, and which make the choice available to everyone:

- using thumbs-up or thumbs-down signs

- sitting or standing on a mat with a happy face (for likes) or a sad face (for dislikes)

- putting a bean in a jar marked 'yes' or a jar marked 'no'.

Once the children are used to offering their views, you can start to gather more diverse opinions by using the following methods:

- **Graffiti walls** – a pattern of bricks, drawn on large sheets of paper, where children can both write their own views, read the views of others, and expand on exciting comments.

- **Suggestion boxes** – these are always available so that comments can be added at any time, as they occur to the children, and not only during fixed consultation exercises.

- **Photo-stories** – children take pictures and add captions.

- **Photo-tours of the nursery** – pictures can be sorted and arranged to show preferred areas and activities.

- **Role-play** – children can role-play discussions and sessions, either imagined or previously held, in order to share their views, change the course of what has happened or create new endings.

- **Evaluations using questions on large sheets of paper** – children can tick what they agree with or add their comments.

- **Key words** – these encourage children to complete sentences with their own words, respond to the views of others, or react to certain words or phrases.

These methods – which are good for children of all ages – are particularly useful when working with a large group of children, as they can be part of circle time.

The strength of this technique is that even very young children can take part. The simple yes/no technique is extremely good for getting simple information and can be a relatively quick way of testing views.

Its weakness is that, when first used, younger children may simply copy each other or try to please the adult running the exercise. Over time, however, children are likely to feel better about expressing their own views, even if they are different to their friends. Children who always seem to hold

> The various methods suggested here have been used successfully on many occasions and new adaptations are being added all the time or suggested by children. For example, staff at a nursery reported how a child with very poor language skills, and some restrictions to his movement, refused to take part in a sorting and building activity which had been moved to a new position in the nursery. He kept knocking the blocks away. Eventually, staff realised that there wasn't anything wrong with the activity itself: the problem lay in the fact that only two children could access the new location at any one time. They interpreted the child's rejection of the activity as expressing a desire either for more space or for more playmates. They also concluded that they had made too many changes at one time. They decided to try out different locations and observe the children's responses.

minority views may need to be supported so that their views are respected and so they don't feel like outsiders.

Even children with profound disabilities have ways of signifying what they like or dislike, though some of the more active methods may need to be adapted to suit a child's individual skills. Getting more detailed opinions may require interpretation.

Ranking preferences

In this technique, children choose pictures from magazines or drawings which represent various alternatives. The pictures are displayed, and the children rank the pictures in order of their preferences. This is a very effective way of finding out what children would prefer when choosing play equipment, arranging an outing or planning meals. The children can vote for their preference by putting up their hands or sticking markers on top of their choices. (A step-by-step approach to using this technique appears under 'Ideas for giving children choice', p. 27.)

This technique can be used in order to get an instant picture of what the group feels, but you can also give the children some time to think about their response.

When using this technique, adults must plan how to explain the majority

A nursery in north London enabled children who attended their extended-day group to choose equipment for their out-of-hours room by asking them to rank their preferences. When the children were reminded that some babies would be there, the older children were able to share out the total amount of money available on age-appropriate toys and games. After this successful pilot, the work was extended so that children throughout the nursery were involved in choosing a proportion of the new equipment.

decision to those who don't agree with it and ensure that some children do not feel that their views are always in the minority.

The strength of this approach is the ability to show children the actual choices available in picture format. Its weakness is that children may still need to have some parameters set for them, a problem that can be overcome by restricting options to what is affordable.

A picture-ranking exercise like this works for all sighted children who can express preferences, but you may need to create verbal 'pictures' and describe the alternatives in detail for children with limited vision.

Mapping

This technique involves the children in drawing or making a model of the way things are now and how they would like them to be. There are several possible ways of carrying out this kind of consultation, and some of them are outlined in the box 'Mapping techniques'.

Mapping is very good for provoking discussion, and it can be used with all children.

The strengths of mapping are that you can use so many different formats and that it allows you to get a lot of information. It also engages children's creativity and senses.

Its weaknesses are that adults need to prepare well and also consider how they will record the children's views and the final product, which can take up a lot of wall space. You also need to allow plenty of time in one session or over an intense few days, as it is hard to come back and recreate the same views and feelings after a gap.

The activities can all be adapted for children with sensory impairment, in order to play to their strengths and capabilities. Some children may need interpreters to help them to express their views.

Mapping techniques

These can be purely exercises of fantasy to engage children's imagination or used to plan real spaces within nurseries or outside play areas.

The island
Draw a large island on sheets of paper. Sit the children around the edge to draw, for instance, their favourite play activity on their part of the island, leaving the middle free. Ask the children to decide which of the items they would move to higher ground if the water was rising. This promotes discussion about individual versus group choices. It is a technique which has been used successfully with young refugees, or children who have had to move house a lot, to discuss what they were forced to leave behind and how they can gain from sharing resources supplied by others.

Memory trail
Display all the information you want children to assess and encourage them to move around, look at it all and then express their opinions.

Draw your ideal park / playground / nursery
Using a workshop approach, ask children to plan a fantasy park or playground. They can use blank paper or pre-drawn templates of the equipment (for example, benches, slides and climbing frames) and/or the setting, decide what to include or exclude and where everything should go. They can also draw their own ideas and create new additions such as a children's zoo or mini-beast area, and these can be moved about before settling on preferred locations.

Sensory walk
Children are taken on a 'journey' and asked to describe what they see, hear, smell, touch or taste. You can record the discussion during the journey on a tape-recorder or talk about it as soon as the children return while the memories are fresh in their minds. If you go for the second option, encourage the children to talk as they walk, to help them have clearer memories of what they have seen. The adults who accompanied them can use prompts to remind them of the route they took but should not supply sensory information.

continued opposite

---

continued from previous page

Case study

In a joint Save the Children / Children's Society project – *London on Your Doorstep*, carried out in 2001 – children aged two-to-four-years were involved in sensory walks and in taking photographs of their local area. They described what they liked and disliked, what was helpful and what wasn't. This information was fed into consultations being held by the Greater London Authority on their strategies for housing, transport and the environment, showing that even the youngest children could participate. The sort of comments that were used to reflect children's views included: "I hear sounds in the park," (on ambient noise); "I saw a lot of rubbish on the floor," (on municipal waste); and, "Is it for big children?" (on city living).

Ideas for giving children choice

The following ideas for running semi-formal consultations emerged during staff training sessions as part of the CHOOSE project. They use simple techniques that have been outlined above, and show how easy it can be to enable very young children to express clear opinions. In each case, we outline the process or approach and some methods that can be used.

Buying toys and equipment

1 Select three suitable items of play equipment from a nursery equipment catalogue. Ensure that all three are in stock and can be delivered fairly promptly following an order.

2 Make enlarged copies of the three pictures in the catalogue.

3 Stick each picture on a big jar and put the three jars somewhere accessible to all or most of the children. Encourage the children to describe what is on the jars to each other, and to include any children with visual impairment in this discussion.

4 If possible, provide a number of objects which are made of similar material to the three toys so that all the children can tell what the toy might feel like. Other sensory experiences can help illustrate a toy and will make choice accessible to more children, both disabled and non-disabled. For example, give children a hand fan to create wind in their faces as a way to illustrate one feature of going down a slide.

5 During the period when the children are looking at the pictures on the three jars, encourage them to talk about the toys. Ask them what they like about them, and how they think they might use them. This needn't be a heavy-handed process. You can do it with children as they are looking at the jars (individually or in groups), or simply as part of the general chat that goes on while the children are engaged in other activities.

6 Once everyone has had a look at the pictures, ask each of the children to put a wooden bead in the jar representing the toy they like best. This needn't be done in one session or even in one day. Some children may need more time to make up their minds than others, and it is good to consult the children who attend the setting on a part-time basis too. The process could take a whole week or maybe more, though it should not stretch out so far that the children who voted early lose contact with the activity.

7 During the voting period, it is a good idea to find ways of discussing the fairness of majority choice with the children and to talk about the issues involved if some children always find themselves in the minority.

8 At the end of voting, count all the beads and give the children the result of the choice they have made.

9 Order the chosen equipment as soon as the result is in, chase the provider if it does not arrive promptly and let the children know what you are doing.

Going on an outing

1 Talk to the children about what an outing is while looking at pictures of previous outings.

2 Select two possible excursions which are similar in terms of the distance to be travelled, the complexity of planning and management and the level of excitement they are likely to generate in the children. So, an afternoon playing unusual games in the local park might be offered alongside a visit to storytelling at the library, while a trip to the zoo could be offered against a visit to the fire station. Ensure that all possible destinations are accessible to all the children, and appropriate to their abilities.

3 Make two wall displays using pictures of children enjoying themselves at these locations.

4 At the same time, find ways of illustrating the two destinations using materials that can appeal to other senses. For instance, a large bag of freshly-mown grass might evoke the sense of being outdoors in the park and a tape of stories can help the children understand the excitement of stories told by professionals.

5 Individually, in groups and during normal play, talk to the children about the pictures on display. Some children will have been on these excursions with family or friends, and you can encourage them to share their experiences with the others. Reading stories set in each of the destinations will also help general discussion.

6 When all the children have had time to choose, ask them for their preference and put a photo of each child on the wall display illustrating the place they wish to visit. The destination with the most faces wins.

7 Take photographs of the children during the outing and use them to help build a repertoire of photos and souvenirs to illustrate various choices.

Employing several techniques in one consultation

The wide-ranging consultation about outdoor preferences undertaken at Anansi nursery (see page 5) offered all the children different opportunities to express their preferences. It enabled children of different ages, skills and abilities to understand what they were being asked and to respond in a meaningful way. The aims of the exercise were to:

- consult the children and promote their participation in developing the outdoor play area

- identify the children's preferred outdoor play activities

- plan with the children the physical layout of the outdoor provision

- bring about physical change to the environment

- provide the very best outdoor environment for all young children.

The children's views formed the basis for changes to the physical environment, management of the outdoor area and a review of the setting's policy on outdoor play. They were consulted in the following ways:

1 The children watched a video of the garden, and their comments were noted down.

2 The children were encouraged to touch and play with materials and toys already in the garden both in and out of context, alongside materials not in the garden. The materials and equipment provided included:
- bamboo, stones, soil, pebbles, gravel and leaves
- plants, bark, long grass and sand
- weather vane
- tunnel, tyres, logs, hidey holes
- fibre-optic light set in coloured concrete
- shallow pool, mirrors, bridge, water wheel, net and rope
- bird boxes

- area for planting flowers and herbs
- mini beast area.

3 The children's spoken preferences were noted, as well as any other signs of choice, including the length of time they spent with particular materials or the frequency with which they returned to them. Children with limited verbal skills were able to sign some of their preferences or were observed as they reacted to the choices presented to them. Videos and audiotapes were made of play sessions, visits to other play areas and discussions groups. They were played back to these children and to the larger group, to remind them of what had been said, and to see if views had changed or if they had more ideas to add. Two maps were presented to children on the floor and various pictures used in the consultation were shown to each child individually. Discussions focused on specific areas where decisions could be made: play equipment, play surfaces, planting in the garden areas, siting of seats and places for quiet play, activity areas for bikes, places for climbing and hiding. Using pictures from visits or cut out of catalogues, and samples of materials that could be used, the children mapped each area and discussed the various merits of the different layouts, surfaces, textures and smells. This worked best in the garden itself so children could make the leap from map to reality more easily. It was explained to each child what the maps represented, what the process of consultation would be and how a consensus would be reached. Some took time or needed guidance to look at the map and the pictures before making a decision. Others were able to become involved more quickly. The children's views were written down and preferences were recorded on bar charts.

4 Written records were kept of individual and group choices across the various methods of consultation. The results were presented in graphs and displayed in the children's play area. The group found that it was crucial for these results to be recorded systematically and in some

detail. In their choice of pictures, the children showed that they had a preference for:

- bright colours
- natural objects such as wood and flowers
- familiar objects
- ground markings such as numbers
- garden features with shapes such as circles and squares
- textured surfaces.

5 The children got feedback at circle time and in individual discussion, video, graphs and maps. Staff members showed the children which items they had jointly selected for the garden as a result of the consultation. These included skipping ropes, a rope bridge and swings, flowers and plants, tunnels, slides, swings, tyres and bushes.

The Foundation Stage – implications for choice

The curriculum guidance for the Foundation Stage (Qualifications and Curriculum Authority, 2000) is an essential tool for early years practitioners and managers. It complements the early learning goals which should not be seen as 'stand alone' targets in isolation from the guidance.

The guidance is designed to be useful in the full range of settings where three-to-five-year-olds are to be found. It is based on the premise that all children should be given the opportunity to experience the best possible start to their education, and seeks to support the development of early communication, literacy and numeracy skills which will prepare young children for Key Stage 1 of the National Curriculum. It also stresses that the curriculum for the Foundation Stage should underpin all future learning by supporting children's personal, social and emotional well-being, and fostering positive attitudes towards their learning, social skills and persistence.

All the processes involved in consulting young children can contribute to their progress along the stepping stones towards the early learning goals in the Foundation Stage curriculum.

While there is much to be celebrated in this guidance, a curriculum with stated goals may lead practitioners, parents and children to put insufficient value on children's achievements if they do not achieve those goals, especially if they are rigidly interpreted. As soon as achievement is measured by targets, a disabled child – and by implication *any* child who finds a target difficult to meet – is put in a position of disadvantage. In this way, the Foundation Stage has raised particular concerns for disabled children and those with other forms of special educational need.

- The goals may lead practitioners to focus on what the children cannot do rather than on their achievements.

- Over-emphasis on planning may lead practitioners to neglect what children bring to the learning situation; there may be a loss of spontaneity and lack of attention to the children's wider experience or to the barriers that they have overcome as well as to their choices and preferences.

- The primary focus may be on early identification of difficulties rather than attempts to adapt to children's needs.

- Play may be neglected in favour of formal learning for all children, and formal learning may be imposed on children inappropriately. (There is anecdotal evidence, for example, of disabled children being excluded from the literacy hour where teaching strategies are sometimes formal and over-prescribed.) This could be particularly detrimental to disabled children who will always be playing 'catch up'.

- Children may be 'included' but may actually feel marginalised or be physically separated.

Having identified the problems for disabled children inherent in the early learning goals, we are still left with the fact that they provide the framework for early learning and development. Given this reality, it is important to ensure that any activity – whether part of a consultation or not – can be adapted to an individual child's needs, abilities and stage of development. Activities designed in this way make it possible to include positive steps towards the early learning goals for all children, including those with complex and multiple disabilities. Not everyone can reach the goals, but everybody's achievements towards them can be immediately celebrated, recorded and built on in future activities.

3 Involving parents

The focus of this publication is to help practitioners consult young children, and to ensure that disabled children are fully involved in that process. However, real inclusion can only be achieved if all stakeholders are involved with early years settings to some degree. Children, parents and practitioners should be regularly consulted and their views acted on in a meaningful way. This is good for everybody but it is vital if disabled children are to be fully included. Any setting wishing to focus on the interests and entitlements of young disabled children must accept that they will have to make some

institutional and organisational changes. Many of these changes will only work well if all the children, parents and practitioners are part of their planning and implementation processes.

For many settings there are practical barriers to the involvement of parents which need to be overcome. For example, the working conditions of many parents can make it difficult for them to find the time to take part in activities or attend meetings. When disabled children attend a designated rather than a local setting they are often collected by a bus so that parents do not come to the setting on a daily basis and are therefore much harder to reach.

The reasons for working closely with parents of disabled children are much the same as for working with all parents. However, it is important to understand that the experiences of this group of parents, and the context in which they are parenting, may be significantly different to those of a family with a non-disabled child.

Parents of disabled children are sometimes alienated by the amount and quality of professional intervention they have already received. They can seem over-protective and anxious for their children. Remember that previous experiences may have given rise to these worries and insecurities, even if you occasionally feel justified in considering parents' reactions inappropriate.

All settings should be able to establish some degree of parental involvement and communication, especially if they can be flexible and ingenious. Informal social events, held at appropriate times can be an excellent way of 'hooking' parents into more serious planning issues. Anansi Nursery, for example, has a 'graduation' ceremony for their 'leavers', to which all parents are invited. It is always well attended because it has a particular appeal for the parents of that target group. (See page 42 for more on consulting staff.)

Successful collaboration with parents requires an active, on-going commitment to this key relationship. Consultation works best when practitioners make use of the following basic principles:

- Assume that parents will be interested in the opportunity to express their views.

- Value the perspective they bring: their knowledge of their child's abilities, character, life experiences, needs, likes and dislikes.

- Work towards a shared understanding with parents, as this reduces the likelihood that children will receive mixed messages (though remember that home is not an extension of the nursery and parents may not wish to follow all the same practices at home).

- Identify all the ways that parents can be involved in supporting participation, and inform everyone of these opportunities, including those who you know will not have the time to be involved.

- Ensure that parents put themselves forward for involvement; they should not be selected by staff or others.

- Where parents choose not to be actively involved in consultations, ensure that they are given regular feedback on progress.

- Establish mechanisms for parents to get further information on progress or to raise issues or concerns.

- Avoid jargon and make sure your information is parent-friendly.

- Ensure that you are genuinely involving parents, fathers as well as mothers, or any other adult who may be the child's principal carer.

The box overleaf describes how parents were consulted during the CHOOSE project, and offers some simple ideas that you could adapt to your own purposes.

Consulting parents

For both Anansi Nursery and the John Smith Centre, parents were given leaflets about the CHOOSE project, letting them know who would be visiting the settings and what was planned. The parents were also given contact-staff and phone numbers so they could discuss the work.

While the CHOOSE project aimed to foster inclusion, particular efforts were made to ensure that the parents of disabled children understood what was happening. The children's key workers, who knew the parents, talked them through the proposed programme.

At Anansi, programme workers attended a parents' meeting early in the planning stage. While there was interest in the project, no concerns were raised. However, staff felt that this made it easier later on for them to involve parents in changes resulting from the work.

At John Smith, leaflets were produced in minority languages to ensure that all parents had the same information. Project workers were available at the end of the nursery day to meet parents and answer any questions. In fact, no concerns were raised.

4 Staff training and support

We have looked in detail at why young children should be consulted and at the many ways in which you can help them express their views in an inclusive setting. But none of this will get very far without a clear commitment to ensuring that all staff have the skills to engage in these consultations. Involving staff in planning consultations with children and managing the changes that follow are also important for success.

During the CHOOSE project, staff at both Anansi Nursery and the John Smith Centre were offered a training programme (see outline below). The training involved all staff and dealt with issues of inclusion and the benefits of involving very young children in planning and decision-making.

Other settings could arrange appropriate training programmes for themselves along similar lines. This training could be delivered by local

authority training officers, special educational needs co-ordinators (SENCOs) or outside specialists in disability awareness and participation training. Choice of trainers will depend on availability, partnership arrangements and local situations.

Outline content for staff training

No two settings are alike, and the training needs of staff will differ from one organisation to another. Staff in a setting with a strong inclusive tradition are less likely to need background information on the principles behind inclusion than staff working in a setting where inclusive practice is new. The areas suggested below are intended as a guide to the range of skills and knowledge that staff in inclusive settings will need if they are to conduct successful consultations with all the children they work with. Individual settings can choose what they need and build the training plan that suits their needs. They may, of course, wish to cover other issues as well as those listed.

The outline for issues to be covered in staff training is divided into two sections, one on the underlying principles behind inclusive practice and consulting young children, the other on related policy and practice.

Principles

I General background
 • What is anti-discriminatory practice and how can we implement it in settings?
 • What do we think about childhood and children in our society, and from where do we get our ideas about children?
 • How do young children differ from older children?
 • What is a children's rights perspective and how does it impact on policy, planning and practice?
 • What are the barriers and drawbacks to involving children in planning, and what positive opportunities may be created by doing so?

2 Disability awareness and inclusion
- What is disability?
- The history of disabled children and adults.
- The legal context – past and present.
- What is inclusion?
- Inclusion and children's rights.
- How does it feel to be excluded or marginalised?
- The sources of self-esteem for young children.
- How to help disabled children and their families build self-esteem.
- What do disabled adults have to say?
- What is inclusion?
- Case studies and examples of inclusive practice.

Policy and practice

1 Listening to children and communicating with them
- Principles behind tuning in to young children, listening to what they are really saying, and communicating with them.
- Specific methods for communicating with disabled children.

2 Consulting young children
- Key principles behind running a consultation.
- Consultation techniques.
- Designing a consultation.
- Consulting parents.

3 The Foundation Stage curriculum and early learning goals
- General principles of the curriculum.
- Problems raised by the curriculum for disabled children.
- Implications for implementing the Foundation Stage with all children.

4 Making activities accessible to all, and adapting activities to suit individual needs

5 Designing a mission statement

Consulting staff

Practitioners who have benefited from the training listed above should have all the skills and knowledge needed to run inclusive consultations with young children. But a fully inclusive setting will go one step further, and involve these practitioners in the development and planning for a setting so that the consultations they run have a long-term context.

Principles for effective consultation with staff

- Staff should be valued for the range of experience, skills and individual perspectives which they bring. They should be able to comment on areas outside their immediate fields of influence.

- The culture and structure of staff teams and meetings should encourage individuals to feel comfortable about expressing their views openly.

- Managers need to be aware of the advantages of staff consultation and be willing to listen and 'share power'.

- Staff insights and the experiences of individual families can be a significant resource to enable appropriate ongoing development and adjustment.

- It is important to work with all staff: managers, nursery officers, cooks, students, trainees and volunteers. Everyone who wishes to should be able to take part.

- Staff should be able to work together within a range of different structures, not just within team training or team meetings. One example would be to form time-limited sub-groups to work with children and parents on issues, and report back to the whole team.

- It may also be important to find out about what staff do outside work, or experiences they have had prior to joining the current team. Sometimes people have hidden skills, experience and contacts which can be useful.

- Managers can pick up on further training and support needs through supervision.

- Managers should attempt to help the team reach a consensus on changes that are needed and avoid leaving individual staff members with a sense that their views are less useful or valid.

- Where some staff members have reservations or concerns, changes should be piloted and reviewed, so that all staff can be brought on board.

Conclusion

We hope that this guide demonstrates that much can be done within early years settings to help disabled children develop decision-making skills, and that the activities and strategies highlighted can be used to help *all* children to participate in whole-group decisions.

Inclusion is a journey and process which benefits all involved – children, staff and parents – as well as addressing all children's right to be consulted on matters that affect them and government guidance on meeting the entitlements of children with special educational needs.

The principle benefits from adopting an inclusive approach arise from valuing what a child can do rather than focussing on obstacles and difficulties. All children (and adults) face challenges in arriving at shared decisions, but this should not mean that we cease to try to overcome these problems.

We believe we have demonstrated that, by having an open mind and using the skills held by experienced staff who work within early years, innovative and exciting solutions can be found to the potential problems of participation. The only essential resources are the ability to listen to children and a creative response to the challenges raised by children's desire to be heard. Once again the difficulties lie not with the disabled child, but with society's ability to adapt and change. A good place to begin this process is by *Starting with Choice*.

References

Dickins, M with Denziloe, J (2003) *All Together: How to create inclusive services for disabled children and their families*, second edition, National Children's Bureau

Fajerman, L, Jarrett, M & Sutton, F (2000) *Children as Partners in Planning*, Save the Children

Flack, M (1996) 'The usual suspects', *Special Children*, issue 97, pp. 11–13

Kidsactive (2000) *Side by Side: Guidelines for inclusive play*, Kidsactive

Mehrabian, A (1971) *Silent Messages*, Wadsworth

Miller, J (1996) *Never Too Young*, Save the Children & National Early Years Network

QCA (2000) *Curriculum Guidance for the Foundation Stage*, Qualifications and Curriculum Authority

Reiser, R, Chapman, M & Skitteral, J (2002) *Inclusion in Early Years: Disability equality in education course book*, available from Disability Equality in Education, www.inclusiononline.co.uk

Sebba, J with Sachdev, D (1998) *What Works in Inclusive Education*, Barnardo's

Audit Commission (2002) *Special Educational Needs: A mainstream issue, report*, Audit Commission, www.audit-commission.gov.uk

Daycare Trust (1998) *Listening to Children. Young Children's Views on Childcare: A guide for parents*, Daycare Trust